Reading in the
furious fast lane

Reading in the furious fast lane

Fryderyk Von Battenburg

Copyright © Fryderyk Von Battenburg

All rights reserved. No part of this book may be reproduced in any form or by any electronic or mechanical means, including information storage and retrieval systems, without permission in writing from the publisher, except by reviewers, who may quote brief passages in a review.

ISBN: 978-1-64570-206-1   (Paperback Edition)
ISBN: 978-1-64570-207-8   (Hardcover Edition)
ISBN: 978-1-64570-205-4   (E-book Edition)

Some characters and events in this book are fictitious. Any similarity to real persons, living or dead, is coincidental and not intended by the author.

This book may have changed since publication and may no longer be valid. The views expressed in this work are solely those of the author and do not necessarily reflect the views of the publisher, and the publisher hereby disclaims any responsibility for them.

Book Ordering Information

Phone Number: 347-901-4929 or 347-901-4920
Email: info@globalsummithouse.com
Global Summit House
www.globalsummithouse.com

Printed in the United States of America

CONTENTS

1 Time on My Hands 1
2 She's Only a Doll 4
3 Mrs. Long and Herbert 10
4 The Letter 19
5 The Big Score 25
6 This Was a Good Neighborhood 30
7 Robert 36
8 He's Drinkin' Again 46
9 Having a Drunk for a Dad Sucks 48
10 I Can't Decide 50
11 Terra and Firma 54
12 Aliens in the Hill Country 59

About the Author 63
About the Book 65

1

Time on My Hands

I don't suppose that any of you know who I am. My name is Johnny Caruso. I am seventeen years old. For reasons unknown to you, I suspect that turning eighteen years old might create some problems for me. I will legally become an adult. Adults are a very special class of people… and very interesting.

Excuse me for a second. That's Mildred over there. She is rather preoccupied with my health. Listen to what she is saying now. She just can't stop talking.

"Mr. Caruso, you look chipper today! How was your sleep? How are you feeling?" Now she is looking out the window. She continues to talk to me. She never stops. But honestly, I am not paying any attention to her at all. I am trying to compose my thoughts so that I may tell you something that will be of some value to you.

Excuse me again! Some guy is serving us lunch. Let's see: green beans, carrots, mashed potatoes and gravy, and meatloaf. Wait, the guy is actually talking to me. Listen to this!

"I hope you enjoy your lunch, Mr. Caruso. If there is anything else that I can get for you, please let me know. My name is Jason."

Jason walks away from me. He does not turn back to even look my way. All those utterances are a well-rehearsed, meaningless script. What a lame excuse for service.

Now, I have to say that you and I don't have much time to talk with each other, so let's get busy!

I have prepared a "Teenager's Bill of Rights." If you look at things my way, it will all make sense. I hope that I can discuss all of this in a small space of time.

First, all teenagers come from God. Now, I know that may grab you as something odd or funny, but it's the basic premise from which I will explain all else. God gives teenagers their lives. Our lives are fertile gardens in which we may plant a daffodil or an oak. Our garden may be overgrown with weeds. Our garden may be full of rocks. Our parents nurture us as our garden grows, but the final garden is ours—ours! Do you hear me? And that garden might not be real or logical to anyone else.

I think I am going on too long. You might not have that much time, so let's make this quick.

Second, a teenager's life is fragile like a glass vase: clear to all but easy to break. I am not made of steel. I break. I break, for I am only flesh and bone. Handle me with care. Say nice things to me too. Laugh with me. Encourage me to weed my garden and grow flowers and oaks there.

I say this to all teenagers—

Wait! There are some people rushing into my room. Excuse me. They are talking so loud. How rude! "His pulse is dropping! It's a palpable thirty. His rate on the EKG is bradycardia and he is hypoxic. Get me some atropine! Call a code! I am going to intubate him!"

Funny, I didn't think that leukemia was all that bad. I can't finish our conversation now. There's someone by my bedside. He says he is an angel and that we are going on a trip. I told him that I am Johnny Caruso. He says he knows. He's been waiting for me. I told him that I am only a teenager. In fact, you and I are both only teenagers.

Take care.

THE END

2

She's Only a Doll

Yes, it's true that I was born in Hungary—in Budapest, in fact, in 1933. My parents were Dr. Solomon Szennes and Rachel Szennes. Yes, I was born during the time period known as Shoah. What do I remember? I remember that I disobeyed my father and left my mother to save Miriam. Who's Miriam? Please, give me time, and I'll tell you!

My uncle, Israel, said it all started with King Bela IV's Charter of Privileges of 1251, which granted legal status to Jews and gave all of us personal security and the right to practice our religion.

"King Bela's Charter of Privileges was very important!" Uncle Israel would shout, and then he would grab his coat lapels and stand with his legs apart. "King Bela's Charter allowed us Jews to become servants of the Royal Chamber, which was the treasury to which Jews paid their taxes directly. We had the beginning of a defined legal status here in Hungary."

"Israel," my father interrupted, "the Jewish people came here with the Romans when this place was Pannonia, a province of Rome!"

"Solomon, I know that! But where was our legal status? Sure, Romans had legal status. Laws are important. With laws, we are safe, Solomon!"

My father shouted, "Bela Kohn believed in laws, and where is he? The White Terror was horrible! I have never been a Communist. But where were Bela's laws then? And now, think of it, Israel: with the First and Second Jewish Laws of Hungary, you have lost your job. And me… I'm lucky to work!"

"You're lucky. We are all lucky, Solomon! Our Jewish community has a good social aid program. But even I admit that Budapest is getting a little more crowded every day."

My mother said, "Enough politics! It's always politics. And on an empty stomach. Come eat, you two."

I didn't know what it all meant. I was so young, and the world was always wonderful for me. I remember my mama's cooking—goulash and paprika. I guess I didn't know any more than that. What do children know?

But years later, I learned that Hungary had joined the Axis powers—Germany, Italy, and Austria—to try to retrieve lands lost to other countries in the Great War, which some would refer to as World War I. Hungary's lost lands were Transylvania, Slovakia, Yugoslavia, and Ruthenia.

I remember Dohany Street. People were constantly coming to our neighborhood. The streets were so crowded. The smell of paprika was everywhere, and I remember it to this day.

Everyone loved my father, and everywhere we went, he saw his patients. My father lived for his patients. He always made me promise to take care of my mother and never leave her side when he was away. I would promise never to leave Mama's side. People treated my family well.

And then, suddenly, everything changed. The Third Jewish Law of Hungary was passed, and the war came home to my family. My relatives from the Backa region fled to Budapest. My uncle Israel died fighting the Soviets.

My father continued to practice medicine, even after Miklos Kallas became Hungary's Prime Minister. Kallas hated Jews and called for the confiscation of all Jewish property. It was then that my father began to talk less and less, until he just stopped talking.

In October—or was it September?—of 1944, the Arrow Cross Party took over power in Hungary, and my family was sent to a central ghetto in Budapest. It was there that I, Hanna Szennes, suddenly began my adult life at the age of twelve.

The German trucks came for us one evening. Men with guns ran through our building, shouting for us to gather our belongings, because we were being moved again to make room for good Hungarians.

I whispered to my mother as we leaped unto the truck, "I can't leave Miriam. I've got to go back for her."

"She's only a doll. She will be all right."

"No, she won't be all right, Mama. She's my only sister!"

"Hanna, do you see that German flag? This little patch of Budapest is no longer ours."

The adults were all singing as the trucks moved off into the night. I slid off the truck and rolled into a culvert. It was the last time I saw my mother. I would later learn that she had perished in a death march to Austria.

I knew the way home, because my father had taken me with him on house calls. It is amazing to think that making house calls saved my life. I found my brush, a candle, and a cup. I even found soap that floated in water. Miriam was safe. I placed her into my clothes. Every day, Miriam and I avoided the soldiers. Miriam was a good companion. She never complained.

Later, I found out that my father had survived the war too. He died in Hungary after World War II. I then immigrated to Israel.

It was a very long time ago, and I know that the names and places mean nothing to some. But this was my childhood, so very long ago in Hungary.

THE END

Story Notes for "She's Only a Doll"

Hungary: a landlocked country in central Europe, bordered by Austria, Slovakia, Ukraine, Romania, Serbia, Croatia, and Slovenia

Hanna Szennes: a Hungarian patriot and resistance fighter of World War II, betrayed to and executed by the Nazis

King Bela: King of Hungary from 1061 to 1063 and a member of the Arpad Dynasty

Bela Kun: a Hungarian Communist politician who ruled Hungary for a brief period in 1919 and leader of the Aster Revolution

The White Terror (Hungarian Terror): retaliation carried out against Leftists and Jews by irregular and semi-regular detachments in Hungary in 1919-1920 after the fall of the Hungarian Soviet Republic

Axis powers: those nations opposed to the Allies during the Second World War

Pannonia: an ancient country bounded on the north and east by the Danube, conterminous westward with Noricum and Upper Italy, and southward with Dalmatia and upper Moesia

Dohany Street Synagogue: the largest synagogue in Europe and the second largest in the world

Israel: a country in western Asia on the southeastern edge of the Mediterranean Sea

The Holocaust (Ha-Shoah): the genocide of Jews during World War II by Nazi Germany

Arrow Cross Party: a pro-German, anti-Semitic, fascist party led by Ferenc Szalasi, which ruled Hungary from October 15, 1944, to January 1945.

First, Second, and Third Jewish Laws of Hungary: The first law (1938) restricted the number of Jews in liberal professions, administration, and commerce to twenty percent. The second law (1939) reduced this number to five percent. A quarter of a million Hungarian Jews lost their income. The third law prohibited intermarriage and defined Jews racially.

Miklos Kallas: Hungary's virulent, anti-Semitic prime minister (1942). Kallas ordered that Jewish property be seized by the state, and that the Jews be restricted economically and culturally from Hungarian life. He proposed a final solution to the Jewish question in Hungary.

3

Mrs. Long and Herbert

Mrs. Long was a banker's wife, and it was not unusual that she should occasionally make an investment that involved the acquisition of some property.

Her latest investment had procured a farm of approximately sixty acres, with a small herd of cattle and some chickens. The chickens had not been part of the farm's overall income-producing picture.

Mrs. Long informed her husband about the particulars of their investment. "Joe, according to my report, our flock has approximately eight chickens in it. All of them are hens, and none are pullets. They could all be very healthy if we improved their diet. They could be fed a mixture of corn, salt, bonemeal, fish meal, soybean-oil meal, minerals, and vitamins. All of our hens are capable of laying eggs—except one named Herbert, who, it seems, has never laid an egg."

"How many eggs a year does a hen usually lay, Terri?"

"Approximately 230 to 250 a year, I believe. However, it depends on the hen's nutritional status and age."

"And once the chicken stops laying eggs, then what?"

"Well, most chickens are then sold for meat. Our chickens are rather old and, no doubt, tough, so I suspect that they would be good for stewing. However, I don't think that we will sell them. I will let them live out their natural lives on the farm."

"And why doesn't Herbert lay eggs?"

"I don't know, but I will find out after our visit."

"Well, the report is very interesting, and I think that this piece of property has potential. I hope that you can keep it for a year, and in that time period, perhaps it can be an income-producing property."

"Honey, I hope so."

The drive to the farm did not take long. It was only thirty minutes from Austin by expressway.

Two old pecan trees stood next to an aluminum gate that opened onto a long, winding, sand-colored, gravel road. The lane led up to an old, white, wooden house with a brown roof, which stood in front of a red barn that leaned slightly. A few chickens pecked and scratched in the soil surrounding the farmhouse.

The farm foreman, a man named Bob Abel, stood next to a brand-new Ford pickup truck. He wore blue jeans, a western shirt, and a red cap with white polka dots.

"Good afternoon, Mr. Abel. I'm Terri Long, and I would like to talk with you about this farm. I recently became the owner of it. Can you comment on the report I received about the property?"

"Mrs. Long, this farm has been rather unproductive. The cow herd is small, and we just don't seem to produce many crops out here, because our irrigation system is down. Our only tractor is broken. However, we can run like this for another five years."

"Mr. Abel."

"Please, call me Bob."

"Okay, Bob. Do you work anywhere else?"

"No."

"I notice that you have a new truck."

"Oh yeah, just a little Ford I picked up for the family."

"How can you afford a new truck, a new house, and a new hardware store, when this job pays so little? According to my accountant and this report, there was a great deal of money missing last year."

"I don't know anything about that. What money?"

"Come now, Mr. Abel, you were the only one signing checks!"

"Ah… what checks are you talking about? Let me see those checks."

"Mr. Abel, that's not necessary. You are relieved of your duties as foreman of this farm."

"But, Mrs. Long!"

"Good day, Mr. Abel. And you sir standing next to Mr. Abel are Mr. Johnson, the assistant farm hand? Congratulations, Mr. Johnson. You are the new foreman."

Mrs. Long and Mr. Johnson walked toward the weathered red barn that was surrounded by trees.

"Mr. Johnson, I think that chickens that produce eggs would make this farm more profitable."

"Mrs. Long, the chickens we have here have not been laying for some time."

"Well, you have chickens, and I don't see why they are not laying eggs. The eggs could be sold. I will just have a talk with the chickens and ask them why they are not producing eggs. Do you have a list of their names?"

"Why, no, Mrs. Long. I never inquired about their names."

"Why not? May I ask how many chickens we are talking about?"

"Well, I believe that we have eight chickens, at the last count."

"Eight. Well, surely we can get eight chickens to cooperate."

"Well, Mrs. Long, if you don't mind me saying so, this group of chickens is a rather disagreeable lot. They won't join a union, and I don't think they would vote in any election."

"Well, Mr. Johnson, I don't think there has been much in the way of chicken suffrage, after all."

"Yes, ma'am."

Mrs. Long walked over to the barn and opened the door. "I would like to have all of your names, please," she announced. "I own this farm now, and I think we should meet each other and improve the conditions on this farm for everyone concerned."

The chickens kept pecking and walking around in the barn as if they had not heard a word.

"Perhaps you did not hear me," said Mrs. Long. "I own this farm now, and I think we should meet each other."

"Mrs. Long, this bunch is impossible," said Mr. Johnson. "I think you should sell the whole lot of them."

"Mr. Johnson, I hope that it won't come to that. My feeling is that, with proper nutrition, these chickens would begin to lay eggs. Is that big bird over there a chicken? I don't think I have ever seen such a large chicken. And he doesn't have a comb, does he? That must be Herbert." She called to the big bird, "Herbert, Herbert, come here! Herbert, I am sure that you are an eagle. In all of the books on birds that I have read, your description matches that of an eagle."

"Mrs. Long," said Herbert, "in all honesty, I must remain a chicken. My home is here!"

"Herbert, I respect your wishes, but I simply want to say to you—to set my records straight—that I have seven chickens and one eagle. I respect your wish to remain with your friends, but as an eagle, you have certain abilities that make you unique."

"Unique, Mrs. Long?"

"Yes, unique, Herbert."

"Well, thank you so much, Mrs. Long. Now, if you'll excuse me, it's time for our corn feeding, and I don't want to be late."

"Very well, Herbert."

Mr. Johnson threw the corn at the chickens. Sammy, Bobby, Rollo, Mari, Roxy, and Pollo didn't notice Herbert as he approached the corn scattered on the ground. They were too busy eating.

"Bobby," said one chicken, "what did Mrs. Long want with that misfit Herbert?"

"Who knows? She was probably going to fire him for being a poor chicken!"

At this remark, all the chickens except Pollo began to laugh. Herbert hung his head lower, but he continued to eat the corn.

"Bobby, you are so cruel," said Pollo. "Herbert is a better chicken than you are."

"Oh yeah?"

"That's right."

"If Herbert is such a great chicken, where is his red comb? And why is his beak so large, and his head so big and white?"

"Well, because he is different from you and me."

"That's right. He is different, and we are all the same. He's no real chicken. He's a super-chicken. Ha ha!"

At this remark, all the chickens began roaring with laughter. Herbert moved slowly and held his head even lower. Except for Pollo and Herbert, the chickens eventually drifted away.

"Pollo, why don't I fit in?" asked Herbert. "Why don't I look like everyone else?"

"I don't know, Herbert, but you're okay by me."

"Pollo, what's an eagle?"

"I think it's some kind of bird that represents something ancient."

"What's ancient?"

"Old, I think."

"Well, I couldn't be an eagle then. I am not that old."

"An eagle?" said Pollo. "Don't pull my leg!"

"Well, Mrs. Long informed me that I was an eagle."

"Well, Mrs. Long is wrong. You're a chicken like me. You always have been, and you always will be."

"Herbert, can I talk to you again, please?" asked Mrs. Long. The roaming chickens suddenly stopped pecking and looked over at Mrs. Long and Herbert.

"Herbert, if you and the other chickens start laying eggs, I will give you better food and a new henhouse with a TV and DVD player."

The chickens ran up to Mrs. Long and all began shouting at once. "We are better at laying eggs than Herbert is. His beak is so large he can't dig for worms without making a mess. And his feet are huge."

"Well, I don't know why Herbert's different," said Mrs. Long. "Maybe he is not a chicken. He looks like an eagle."

"I am a chicken," Herbert said. He pecked at the ground.

"An eagle? No way," insisted the other chickens. He's a chicken, just like us."

"Well, okay," said Mrs. Long, "but if you lay eggs, you will have more food, a new henhouse, and a color TV."

As Mrs. Long and Mr. Johnson managed New Heritage Farm, it began to prosper it. The better food made all the animals work harder.

Herbert never laid any eggs, and he was banned from the new henhouse by the other chickens. Pollo, his friend, still visited him. "Mrs. Long is going to have a celebration tomorrow," Pollo told him. "There are posters all over town. I can't wait! There will be a band, balloons, and food."

The day of the celebration came. The farm was decorated with balloons everywhere. Herbert and Pollo walked on the lawn.

"Herbert, look!" said Pollo. "I think I see something on the roof of the water tower!"

"It's Bob Abel," said Herbert, "and he has a BB gun!"

"Why would he have a BB gun?"

"I don't know, but perhaps we should tell someone."

Pollo told Sheriff Moyer about Bob. When the dignitaries had arrived and the dedication ceremony was about to begin, Bob opened fire on the stage, shooting out balloons.

"Herbert," said Pollo, "someone will get hurt if you don't do something."

"What can I do?"

"You're big, Herbert."

"Let's run to the barn," said Herbert. Shots rang out as BBs danced about their feet. "Bob sure is mad!"

"Yes, Bob is mad," Pollo said. His words faded as he slumped over.

Herbert looked at Pollo and tried to shake him, but Pollo didn't move. "Pollo, please speak to me!" He clucked and coaxed, but Pollo still didn't move. He seemed to be asleep.

Herbert held out his wings—a span of approximately seven feet. He looked at his big yellow feet and began to run. He moved clumsily on the ground until his outstretched wings caught the wind, and then he lifted off from the ground. The barnyard below him seemed to grow smaller and smaller. The water tower loomed before him. His keen eyesight picked out Bob and the rifle.

As Herbert soared, he suddenly went into a dive. It was the first dive of his life, and the speed of it frightened him. He couldn't control his speed and almost hit the water tower! He corrected his dive and shot up toward the white clouds above him.

"No one is going to have a celebration today," Bob said to himself. "This is my farm, and I have the last word here!" He pointed the BB gun at Herbert and took aim.

Herbert went into a dive, knowing that he must get the gun. It was now or never. He accelerated, closed his eyes, and wished for the best. At the last moment, he saw the red tower looming before him. Would he miss the gun, or would he succeed? Suddenly he was there, and his outstretched talons grabbed the gun. But Bob wouldn't let go, and suddenly Herbert, Bob, and the gun fell toward the ground. A big haystack cushioned their fall.

The police, who had seen everything, immediately moved in to arrest Bob and take his gun away.

Herbert immediately ran to Pollo, who by now had awakened. "What happened?" Pollo asked.

"Bob was mad because he didn't get the farm," said Herbert. "He wanted to spoil the celebration by shooting the balloons."

"Oh, Herbert!" all the chickens screamed. "You saved the celebration. We didn't know that chickens could fly so high and so fast."

Pollo looked at them and then at Herbert. He said, "Herbert is an eagle, not a chicken. He will always be a member of our family, but he's an eagle, and the sky belongs to him."

"Pollo, I shall live here the rest of my life," said Herbert. "In my heart, I will always be a part of this farm—but as an eagle. I will claim the sky above and all the freedom that goes with it. We are all important, and each of us has his place. To be a chicken is not so bad, and to be an eagle is not so bad, either."

Mrs. Long, who had been at the farm dedication, suddenly ran up to the group. "I see, Herbert, that you really are an eagle—and a brave one, in fact."

"Thank you, Mrs. Long."

"Can we still have the party?" the chickens asked.

"Why, yes!" said Mrs. Long. And suddenly the barnyard was again full of dancing, singing, and much happiness.

On this day, courage and an eagle were born.

THE END

4
The Letter

"I have a better connection now," I said. "You want to know more about the letter? What newspaper are you with? *The London Observer*? No, my father didn't steal the letter! No, I cannot answer questions over the phone right now!"

I replaced the phone in its cradle. Actually, I slammed the phone down. It was the third time this week that someone had called my father a thief and accused me of not being truthful. I hadn't stolen anything.

The elderly lady had given me that letter. She had said, "Please release this letter after my passing. I don't want my letter to be lost forever in the dusty family archives." I hadn't questioned her much. I had simply done what she'd asked.

I was a teenager, enrolled in high school. My father was Dr. Robert Stern, a nephrologist. He was very good with problems of the kidneys. My father had been asked to give a talk in London about a certain kidney disease. I went to London with him, because he promised to take me to the Tower of London to see the crown jewels of England.

During the London medical meeting, my father had been approached by one of his colleagues, who had requested a medical consultation for a patient. In a hushed voice, the man spoke to my father, who listened intently.

It was during this consultation visit that I met the patient.

My father and I were driven to a large, gray building, surrounded by gates and guards. Soldiers in gray coats stood at attention at various stations around the building. A huge flag flew at the front of the building. We walked down a long hallway and then went up a flight of stairs. The walls were covered with oil paintings of people in jewels and crowns. On all the tables were numerous bronze sculptures. The air smelled of fresh-cut flowers, dampness, and the faint aroma of lemon polish.

I sat in a room with many chairs and a couch, all centered around a television set. As I waited impatiently for my father, I got up and opened an adjoining door. It was there I caught a glance of a small, white-haired woman sitting in a bed and facing a window. She seemed asleep or deep in thought. I turned to leave.

"Oh, do come in," she said. "I don't bite."

"I am looking for Dr. Stern. Have you seen him?"

"Well, he is quite popular, so it would seem. I too am waiting for him and Sir Paul."

"Excuse me, but I am his son. He came here to see a patient and promised not to take too long! I wanted to see the Crown Jewels of England at the Tower of London. Have you seen them before?"

"Oh, I see. Well, I am the patient. Upon occasion, I have worn them. Well, don't stand there. You must come in and wait with me."

I walked into the room and sat down. Looking out the windows, I saw a park with trees. I said nothing as I waited quietly. The white-haired woman's pale blue eyes began to look at the wall. I soon realized it was a door. It suddenly opened. A man dressed in a black uniform rushed in.

"Ma'am, I am so very sorry that he is here," the man in the black uniform said. "You there, come quickly with me, now!"

"Do go away," said a woman's voice. "We are waiting for Dr. Stern. We are becoming acquainted with each other. Go away!"

The door closed again. I looked out the window and noticed how dreary the gray, overcast day appeared. It seemed to invade the small room.

"What are you called, young man?" asked the woman.

"Who, me? I am Jonathan Stern."

"Jonathan, I used to be called many things, but now I am just 'ma'am.' If I could get up, I would venture out there for a walk!"

"The weather's terrible out there. It's so comfortable and warm in here."

"That's really the point, isn't it? The cold braces one. It wakes you up and invigorates your senses."

Who would want to go out in weather like this? I thought.

"I adored my father," she continued. "He loved to shoot in weather like this. Oh, darling Papa. Even in weather like this, the boxes never stopped. All I wanted was a home in the country, surrounded by animals, dogs, cows, and horses. I wanted my own home and my own friends! Then Uncle David let that woman come between us. Well, I knew that I was next, and freedom flew out the window as duty stepped in. I was ready—or so I thought. Gangan was there, but I quickly realized that I was not ready. Can I trust you, Jonathan? Or shall my thoughts be lost to some dusty archive?"

"Trust me for what?" I asked, thinking it was a strange thing to say.

"When I have passed, I want you to deliver my letter to the newspapers whose addresses appear on the back of the letter. Keep the original copy, and make copies of this letter. My wishes won't be respected here and now. You're my only hope. Walk over to that desk. In the right upper drawer is an envelope. Take it, Jonathan. Do as I say! Don't be frightened. Good. It's in your hands. Well done. Sit down quickly. Someone's coming."

I later found out who the lady was. Even now, I don't believe it. In one small paragraph of the letter, she had written, "As Princess Elizabeth, I unknowingly became queen while on the slopes of Mount Kenya. I always knew that it was possible, but it came much too quickly. I accepted my fate, and I must tell you now that it was hard. Uncle David rejected who we were, and that I could never do. I ask you, does duty have to be so difficult? I am only human, as all others are. I was asked to go beyond the endurance of the human heart and mind. I lost Lillibet on the way to becoming someone else. Papa would have understood me. To you, my successor, I wish you Godspeed!"

The letter was signed, "Elizabeth R."

THE END

Story Notes for "The Letter"

London: capitol of England

sovereign: ruler, one who exercises supreme authority within a limited sphere

nephrologist: a medical doctor who specializes in diseases of the kidney

Buckingham Palace: the official London home of the English monarch

Crown Jewels of England: precious regalia of the monarchy

Tower of London: an early fortress in central London, where the crown jewels of the English monarchy are securely kept

regina: Latin word for *queen*

Queen Mary: consort of George V, and grandmother to Queen Elizabeth the Second, nicknamed Gangan

archive: place where records or historical documents are stored

regalia: the emblems, symbols, or paraphernalia indicative of royalty

Elizabeth II: the monarch queen of Great Britain from 1953 to present

accession: the act of coming to high office or a position of honor or power

Duke of Windsor: Edward VIII, known to his family as David, who abdicated the English throne in December of 1936 to marry American Wallis Simpson, twice divorced

Margaret McDonald: one of the queen's closet friends, deceased, and one of the few people who could refer to the queen as Lillibet, which was what the queen had called herself as a child because she couldn't say *Elizabeth*

5
The Big Score

"Mom, I did not sell that painting at Old Curiosities. I sold it from the garage. I don't see why I have to share the money with Mr. Gold!"

"Okay, Mister Big Businessman. Your first deal, and you are a fink. I raised a shyster. Everyone will say that my son is a crook!"

"Mom, you overexaggerate everything!"

"Go ahead, buster! By the way, you're late for work!"

Josh Turner, fastest bike in town, raced his red bike through Middlebury's traffic and zoomed down Main Street. Would Mr. Gold find out about the sale of the painting?

Josh was late to work at the antique shop, Old Curiosities. His bike danced unto Middlebury's traffic circle, passing one dangling, weathered traffic light. Josh hoped that Mr. Gold would never find out about the sale of the painting. But what if he did? Josh would be history at the Old Curiosities—no job, no money, no Xbox, no fast-foods ever again. But what did it matter? The deal had netted a tidy profit—not bad for a twelve-year-old boy who worked part-time at a small job in a dilapidated old building in the middle of nowhere surrounded by decay and weeds.

"Show me the money! *My* money!" Josh imagined Mr. Gold saying to him. But Mr. Gold couldn't find out. Josh needed this money. Wally World didn't pay his mom enough to support a family of five people.

David Gold knew the antique business, and it was the same year after year. There was nothing new, and everything in his shop was old. He looked at the quality of the goods he purveyed. People nowadays didn't appreciate quality. In his right hand he held a brass compass, the magnetic needle pointing north. The compass had been made nearly one hundred years ago. Hardly anything modern worked after only five years. He gently placed the compass back unto a mahogany desk. The mahogany had been polished so many times that a golden fire radiated from its surface.

The bell on the front door of the shop rang as the postman entered. David didn't bother to look up. The only thing in the mail these days were bills and more bills, tons of them.

David placed the mail on his desk. He sorted through it, hoping for a letter saying that his uncle Sol had died, leaving him a fortune, or that he had won the lottery. He stood up and threw the bundle of letters on his desk. The door bell rang again, and two well-dressed people walked into the shop.

David Gold jumped to his feet. He adjusted his tie, and a smile appeared on his face. He stood up straight, with good posture. "Good morning," he said. "Welcome to Middlebury's finest antique shop. How may I be of service to you?"

The elderly man with a full head of gray hair began to speak. "We wanted to sell some of our things. Do you buy and sell?"

"Why, yes, I buy and sell only the best! The best only and always!"

The elderly woman standing behind the man began to nudge him forward. "My name is Forest… Benton Forest. I served in Germany in World War II, and I brought back some porcelain pieces. I want to know if you can buy them. I have them with me. I need to sell them today." The man named Forest began to carefully unwrap the brown bundles that he and his wife had carried into the store. "Mr. Gold, you look disgruntled," he said. "There's a frown on your face." Mr. Forest leaned cautiously toward Mr. Gold. "Can you buy these two pieces?"

"Well, Mr. Forest, I see this kind of stuff every day. Copies are everywhere. Do you think that you are the only one who has such things?"

"Well, I was outside of Berlin in 1945. My outfit was looking for a headquarters to establish for the major. The big shot's house where I found this stuff was surrounded by guardhouses and flowers. Can you imagine flowers in the middle of a war? About the time we GIs had arrived, the guards were gone, and the house was empty. Well, sir, I then secured the place—and one good wine cellar—for the major. I also picked up a few souvenirs for the folks back home. These are real from Germany, not copies!"

"How much do you want?" David Gold stood with both hands on his hips. "How much do you need, Mr. Forest?"

"Well, heck, I need a million dollars. But I was hoping to get one hundred dollars for my efforts."

"I will give you one hundred dollars."

Mr. Forest placed his hand on his chin. He looked at the woman, who nodded. "It's a deal."

The Forests left the shop. David knew his customers. Mrs. Adler loved Meissen. She would easily pay ten thousand dollars for each. He carefully placed the treasures into a vitrine. Now, where was the rest of the mail? A letter with red stamps caught his eye. He sat quietly as he mused over this piece of correspondence. Who could be sending him a letter? Uncle Sol? A silver letter opener moved methodically in his hand, and he hummed as he opened the letter and read it.

Dear David,

    I know it has been some time since you and I have spoken to each other, but I couldn't bear the suspense. I have to ask you! Were you the one who found the Parmigianino painting? I have talked to a friend at Sotheby's who says the opening estimate is between nine hundred thousand and one million US dollars. The scuttlebutt is that the painting was found in Middlebury, and yours is the only shop there. This latest painting is going to make *The Madonna with the Long Neck* look like a sketch! Well done! You did it! By the way, when I was last in Florence, I saw Brozino's *Eleanora of Toledo*. I know it's your favorite painting.

Sincerely yours,
Nicholas Strong

    Josh arrived at Old Curiosities. He rolled his red bike in through the front door as the bell rang.

"Explain to me, Josh, why you are always late." Mr. Gold slammed a book down on the desk, knocking a finial off of a lamp. "What is it this time, Josh?"

"I am so sorry for being late." Josh gently picked up the jade finial, hoping Mr. Gold hadn't found out about the painting. "I will stay late for free. It won't cost you a thing, Mr. Gold."

"Oh, Josh, forget it. I am upset that an old business associate of mine is bragging again and trying to rub mud in my face. He said that someone discovered an Italian Mannerist painting worth millions here in Middlebury last week." Mr. Gold looked out the window as he placed his hands on his hips. He turned around with a scowl on his face. "Here! I don't believe it. You and I wouldn't have missed something like that, not in a million years. Not at all. Impossible!"

"Mr. Gold, I didn't miss it," Josh said. "I sold the painting. It was an Italian Mannerist painting by Parmigianino."

"Impossible! You didn't tell me about it? Young man, you have some explaining to do!"

"I sold it to Harper after buying it from Vivian Frick for twenty dollars. Harper paid me twenty thousand for it."

"Josh, the auction estimates are one to two million US dollars for that painting. Harper ripped us off!"

"No," Josh said. "He hasn't won yet. I am going to Mr. Levy, our attorney. He will know what to do. I haven't cashed that check yet, Mr. Gold." Josh rushed out the door.

"This is a fine example of the work of Parmigianino. Do I have a bid for one million? One million five hundred thousand… now one million nine hundred thousand… wait, two million five hundred thousand. Does anyone else want to bid for this lost treasure. Last bid, anyone? Sold to number 234!"

"I am a millionaire, Mr. Gold!"

"We are both millionaires, partner!"

THE END

6

This Was a Good Neighborhood

"Hey, Lenny, I bet I can beat your feathers off in a swim across the lake!" growled Ralph. At three feet tall, Ralph was covered with brown fur from the top of his head to his paws. Brother bear Rene, Ralph's twin, stood next to him as they stared down at Lenny, a twelve-inch-tall Mallard duck.

"Come on, Lenny. Don't let him talk to you that way. He's just taunting you because you're the best swimmer in the forest." Rene laughed.

"No kidding, Rene. I just happen to be a duck, and ducks swim."

Lenny sped across the lake with Rene and Ralph in hot pursuit.

"That's not fair, Lenny," shouted Ralph. "You cheated. Hey, Rene, didn't Lenny cheat? Let's see who can swim *back* the fastest, my little speedboat."

Beneath the water, Rene could hardly contain his laughter as he grabbed Lenny's feet and kept him from moving. Ralph was swimming as fast as he could to the other side of the lake.

"Hey, dude, let me go!" Lenny demanded. "Rene, let me go right now. I'm gonna tell everyone how you tried to get honey and were stung by a million bees. Let go! I gonna tell Tina you like her."

"I don't like Tina," Rene said suddenly, letting Lenny go.

Lenny sped across the lake and managed to beat Ralph by an inch.

"Lenny, you always win our swim contests. But I can beat you running to our house for pizza and sodas!" Ralph ran off into the woods, with poor Lenny waddling to keep up.

"Hey, wait up, Ralph!" yelled Lenny.

"Go ahead, guys. I'll collect our things." Rene climbed out of the lake and began to dry off.

Rene had not noticed the stranger leaning on a tree by the shore. On her shoulder were a yellow canary and a blue parakeet. The stranger hummed a song that seemed familiar, but the sound was distant. "Hey, bear, why do you hang out with a duck?" she asked. "Shouldn't you be *eating* duck? What is wrong with you? Ducks taste like fish—such good eating, and better than the pizza at home." The stranger slowly walked away.

Rene quickly gathered up their belongings.

"Did you see the look on that bear's face?" The lady laughed as she addressed the yellow canary. "I bet he will think twice about hanging out with that Lenny kid. Perplex, did I cause some trouble or what?"

"You said your usual devilish things," answered Perplex, "and I am sure it won't take long before he has roasted duck!"

"And what do you think, Ill Wind?"

"Oh, mistress, it always works. Just spread a few ugly words here and there, and the fun begins. This is more fun than magic, and carefully placed words never hurt. Taking over this forest is going to be so easy!"

"You don't look so good, Rene," said Ralph. "You sick or what? Hey, don't throw up in here. I am not going to explain anything to Mom and Dad!"

Rene went to his bedroom.

"What's up with Rene, Ralph?" asked Lenny. "He looks like he's seen a ghost. Want another piece of pizza?"

"No sweat, Lenny. He gets sick sometimes when he hangs out in the sun too much. He's so un*bear*able." Ralph laughed as he bent over, pretending to be Rene. "What a wimp!"

"Give him a break, dude. It was hot out there. I became a little sick myself. Besides, he isn't here to defend himself. Hey, don't turn the channel. I haven't seen that movie." Lenny wrestled the remote from Ralph.

The next day, Lenny awakened to go for a morning swim. The lake was always quiet in the morning. Lenny was startled when a strange woman with long, stringy, gray hair ran out of the woods, screaming and waving her hands in the air.

"The bears are trying to kill me! The bears are trying to eat me! Run for your lives! Hey, you, duck-boy, run for it! I heard that the bears are planning roast duck for lunch. Did you hear what I said, web-foot? The bears are coming! Run!"

The tall, bony woman ran back into the woods as quickly as she had come out. Lenny noticed a yellow canary following the woman.

Why, that's ridiculous, thought Lenny. *Everyone around here knows that bears only eat berries and fish—and of course, pizza. Roast duck—I don't think so!*

Lenny saw the bears. "Hey, Ralph, Rene! I just saw something totally weird. This strange lady came running through the woods, screaming that the bears are coming."

"Hey, it's not funny, Lenny!" said Ralph. "This lady's gone through the whole forest saying weird things. Rene told me what she said and why he was ill earlier. Did she have a canary with her?"

"Hey, how did you know?" asked Lenny.

"Rene told me. What are we going to do, Lenny? These things being said are causing problems. My brother got sick, and I don't feel so good, either. We've got to do something. What's next, dude?" Ralph lay his head onto his paws.

"It's not that bad, Ralph." Lenny placed a feathered wing on Ralph's shoulder.

"Let's just talk to this lady and tell her to knock off the weird remarks."

Rene, Ralph, and Lenny went to the house where the lady lived.

Lenny stood on Ralph's shoulder and rang the doorbell. The door opened, and the lady appeared, a parakeet and a canary on her shoulder. "Well, if it isn't the three musketeers," she said sarcastically. "What's the duck doing on your shoulder, bear-brain? No doubt, doing your thinking for you. What can I do for you three losers?" The birds laughed hysterically.

"My name is Lenny, and we don't appreciate the things you're are saying around here!"

"So? Whatever!"

"Everyone tries to get along here in this forest. You're causing everyone not to feel good about themselves."

"It's beginning to feel like home," said the lady. "Excuse me, boys, but you have me confused with someone who cares. I do whatever I want to do. As for you, birdbrain, you'd better get off my porch. Now!"

"Ma'am, I am not here to cause trouble."

"Well, I am, duck-boy. Williwamus!" the lady screamed, pointing at Lenny. He suddenly became a plastic duck.

"Did you see that?" said Rene. "She's turned him into a toy duck!"

The woman bent over, picked up Lenny, and went back into the house, slamming the door shut behind her.

"We've got to get Lenny back," said Rene. "We can't just leave him!"

"Look! There's an open window," said Ralph. "Quick! Climb inside!"

The two bears stumbled into a bathroom, where the canary was adjusting the temperature of the bath water and adding bubble bath to the tub. Lenny, now made of plastic, sat on a stool beside the tub. Ralph grabbed the fleeing canary and said, "Bears love canaries. Where are you going so fast? Let's you and me talk about spell reversal! Tell me now, and don't leave out anything, or else you're going to be an appetizer."

"Simply say, 'This spell reverse I,'" said the shaking canary.

Lenny immediately turned back into a living duck. "Wow, I felt so unreal. What happened? Rene, Ralph, what's going on, guys?"

"We'll download you later," said Ralph. "Right now we have some work to do." He turned to the canary. "What does your magic boss hate the most?"

"Well, she hates hip-hop and rap music," said Perplex. "We moved from the last forest because of that."

"Here she comes," Lenny quacked. "Let's get out of here guys." The three of them headed out the bathroom window. "I have a boom box. You get the music."

Lenny, Ralph, and Rene ran around the lady's house. Suddenly, rap music filled the air. The peaceful lull of the forest disappeared with the rhythmic boom of loud lyrics.

The lady ran out of the house, screaming. "What is that racket? This was a good, quiet neighborhood. I'm trying to watch Bewitched. Turn that music down!" The lady began pulling her hair. "Why, this is crazy! You just can't go anywhere and start trouble anymore! Perplex! Ill Wind! Call a realtor. I'm moving!"

Lenny, Rene, and Ralph cheered.

"It worked! It worked!" quacked Lenny. "She's outta here!"

THE END

7

Robert

"I would be delighted to name him, Mrs. Hen," said Mr. Majors. "But how do you know the sex of this chick here?"

"Sir, all mothers know their children. This chick is a boy."

"If you say so, Mrs. Hen. How many chicks did you have?" Although it was polite to inquire, the truth remained that, to Mr. Majors, all the chickens looked alike. Even though Mr. Major's farm was huge—five hundred acres with an unimaginable amount of livestock—he seemed to know each animal and all the things that made the farm run. This knowledge was at Mr. Majors' fingertips. His best friend was Old Blue, his dog. His most trusted adviser was Mrs. Goose.

"Sir, I had ten chicks this time. This chick here is the largest chick in all of the henhouses."

"I would name him Robert," said Mr. Majors. "He is most beautiful. And this chick is going to be a rooster, Mrs. Hen?" A look of consternation crossed his face.

"He's quite a rooster-to-be, sir," she said as she laughed and beamed with pride.

"Well, Robert it is. And my hat is off to you for such a fine-looking boy!"

"Thank you," said Mrs. Hen. She gathered all ten of her chicks and moved into the yard with Robert in the lead.

Mr. Majors considered the differences in the chicks' sizes. Robert was indeed larger than the other chicks. Mrs. Hen was right, after all. Mr. Majors knew there was work to be done, so he headed back toward the farmhouse. The chickens didn't follow him into the yard. He closed the gate to the farmhouse yard and walked up the porch steps.

"Mr. Majors, I do believe that we will need more fried chicken than we had planned," said Mrs. Majors with a laugh. "I've seen you talking with Mrs. Hen in the barnyard. That big chick might be a good addition to our lunch!"

"Hands off!" said Mr. Majors. "I just named that chicken. I want to see him become a fine rooster."

"Him? And how do you know it's a boy?"

"Mrs. Hen told me. I named him Robert."

"You're really a good farmer."

"Thank you."

Robert became the largest chicken in the yard. He was strong, and he had a magnificent comb. Mr. Majors admired him, but the other chickens feared him. The chickens saw that Robert was aggressive and mean. Robert was even calling the other roosters bad names, but Mrs. Hen ignored Robert's name-calling. Robert called others names and encouraged the other chicks to do the same. The rooster in charge of the chicken yard had heard about Robert's cruel tricks, name-calling, and mean behavior.

One of the roosters suggested to Mrs. Hen that Robert should be sent away, and she protested. She thought her Robert was just fine. She wouldn't hear of sending him away.

Rooster Smith, the chicken-yard leader, approached Mr. Majors. "Sir, I have a young chick who is calling names and is causing a general ruckus in our yard."

"What has he called you, Rooster Smith?" Mr. Majors asked.

"He has called me Rooster Spite, and he called my chick Junior Dumplings!"

"Well, sticks and stones may break my bones, but words shall never hurt me," replied Mr. Majors. "Don't take it personally."

Rooster Smith walked away from the gate. Mr. Majors always knew the right thing to do. Rooster Smith would just ignore Robert.

As he turned into the chicken yard, he saw that a dog had broken into the henhouse. This had never happened before. The lock on the gate had been broken. A stray dog had broken in and killed some hens. The remaining chickens now stood waiting for Rooster Smith to explain why this had happened.

At the back of the flock, Robert and his gang of young male chickens booed Rooster Smith. Robert booed the loudest and said, "You're a washed-up old loser! There's no safety here for us."

"Now, everyone, please be quiet," said Rooster Smith. "The gate was left open and a key was found near the lock. I will investigate. Tomorrow, after our investigation, Mr. Majors and I will meet with my son, Junior Smith, and get to the bottom of this tragedy. Okay, that's all."

"Father, there were feathers and chicken tracks near the lock," said Junior Smith. "Only two male chicks have feet that big—Robert and I—and everyone knows that Robert is a liar and a bully. I didn't go near that gate, but I know who did."

"Don't worry. Tomorrow we will both go to Mr. Majors and find out who did this. Go find Mr. Majors now, and tell him what you told me."

Junior Smith walked quickly toward the gate that led into Mr. Majors' yard. He was ambushed by the same dog that had ravaged the chicken yard. The dog bit Junior Smith and broke his neck.

Robert watched from a distance, as the dog carried the lifeless chicken away to his home by the highway. Robert waited for him to come back.

"Now, do I get my meat bone as a reward?" the dog asked in a low growl.

"Sure," said Robert. "Help! Help, Mr. Majors!" screamed Robert. Mr. Majors came out with his shotgun. "There is the dog that killed the chickens!" Robert crowed. The dog began to run as Mr. Majors raised his shotgun and fired. The dog jumped in slow motion and then lay dead.

"Good work, Robert," said Mr. Majors. "I am sorry that Junior Smith is dead. Rooster Smith is going to take this hard. Robert held his head down as Mr. Majors spoke. "But Robert, you're a hero." Robert then held his head up high.

"I will take Junior Smith back to the chicken yard," said Robert somberly.

"Oh, Robert, how kind of you!" said Mr. Majors. "You're not only a hero, but you're modest."

Robert lifted Junior Smith's body with great reverence.

A group of hens ran up to the fence. "Oh, Mr. Majors, Rooster Smith is dying! Come quickly!"

Mr. Majors ran to the chicken yard, where Rooster Smith lay dying. Mr. Majors picked up the dying rooster, who gasped, "The water," as he pointed at the water dish that lay beside him.

Mr. Majors picked up the dish and smelled bitter almonds. "How did this happen?" he asked aloud. "How?"

With his last breath, Rooster Smith whispered to Mr. Majors, "Robert." But Mr. Majors didn't hear him.

"Robert, both Rooster Smith and his son are dead," said Mr. Majors. "You're the new head rooster of this chicken yard." He called the chickens to order. "Hens and roosters, I have good news and sad news. Two of our roosters are dead. Robert is the new head rooster." Mr. Majors walked away.

As soon as Mr. Majors was out of sight, Robert dropped Junior Smith's body and trampled over it, saying, "Later, you useless maggot food!"

The other chickens stood silently as Robert walked into the chicken coop. The young roosters in his gang immediately followed him into the coop. He told them he was making a list of instructions, which he would post on the door outside his coop.

The hens and other roosters shook their head silently as they read the list:

1. Speak to no other chickens from neighboring farms.
2. Report anything negative that is said about this henhouse.
3. Do not play with other animals.
4. Robert, the rooster, is to be obeyed.

One rooster commented that this list was crazy. The next morning, this rooster was found dead from an accident. No one commented out loud again. They were too afraid. The other animals on Mr. Majors' farm noticed that the chickens were no longer friendly. They kept to themselves and chased out any other animals that strayed into the chicken yard.

The chickens kept everything neat and clean. Their efficiency was amazing too, as farmer Majors noticed more eggs. The population of the chicken yard had quadrupled, and there were more roosters than ever before. It was amazing!

The trouble began very slowly. The other animals grew nervous. The chickens seemed to be everywhere the other animals were not. At one time, the cattle had hung out in the east field, and now they didn't. Chickens spilled out of the chicken yard and into the east field, all the way to the meadows where the horses exercised. They spread to the hill where the sheep flocked, and all the way to the pond where the ducks swam. The chickens reached all the way to the pig sties and to the yard where the goats were milked. Mr. Majors didn't complain, because productivity was very high.

"Mother, have you noticed how many chickens there are?" Mr. Majors said to his wife.

"Yes, Father. They all seem bigger too. No little chicks anymore."

The O'Rourke farm was adjacent to the Majors' farm. It had been quiet for years. The O'Rourkes were sheepherders who tended to mind their own business and affairs. Mr. Majors had not seen Mr. O'Rourke in years, so he was surprised to see Mr. O'Rourke approaching his house.

"You killed my sheep," said Mr. O'Rourke angrily. "Your wild dogs destroyed two rams and seven ewes."

"Mr. O'Rourke, we only have one dog on this farm, and he sleeps inside every night!"

"Where did the dogs come from?"

"Heck, I don't know, O'Rourke. You tell me! As I told you, we don't have any dogs here except Old Blue."

"I'm telling you, some dogs killed my sheep!" Mr. O'Rourke turned around and walked to his truck. He drove off very fast.

Mrs. Majors came outside to where Mr. Majors was standing. "Was that O'Rourke? What was that all about? Why was he so mad?"

"I don't know, but something is killing his animals and disrupting the peace. I'm gonna let O'Rourke cool off, and in a couple of weeks, I'll go over to his place and have a look around."

Two weeks later, Mr. Majors found himself on the road to the O'Rourkes' farm. The road was rocky. Mr. Majors navigated over the bumps deftly. The east field was empty except for the chicken that were everywhere. Mr. Majors drove up to the main farmhouse. A "for sale" sign stood out front. Mr. Majors knocked, but no one answered. After a moment, a man came from around the side of the farmhouse and spoke to Mr. Majors.

"Mr. O'Rourke is dead, kicked by a horse. Then a bale of hay fell on the horse and killed it. What a pity. It was Mr. O'Rourke's favorite horse."

"This is all bad news. I hope the next owner will have better luck. This used to be a prosperous sheep farm!"

"There are no more sheep here, mister. This farm has nothing but chickens!"

"But Mr. O'Rourke told me that his farm was a sheep farm."

"If you say so, mister. I am new here, and all I see are chickens. Have a good day!" The man walked away.

Mr. Majors stood quietly for a moment. None of this made any sense. He had to see Mrs. Goose. She was smart, and she always kept her eyes open. He walked back to his car and drove to the little house where Mrs. Goose lived.

"Mrs. Goose, it's Mr. Majors. Might I have a word with you? I have been witnessing some strange things around here, and I need your advice."

"Oh, Mr. Majors, do come in." Mrs. Goose ushered Mr. Majors inside her house quickly. She turned her head from side to side.

"Mrs. Goose, what is happening around here?"

"I can't say! I can't tell you right now. I just can't say!"

"Mrs. Goose, where are all the other animals? Why are there so many chickens everywhere?"

Outside Mrs. Goose's house, a couple of chickens suddenly appeared. Mrs. Goose noticed the two chickens and became more agitated. The chickens stared at her house. "Mr. Majors," she whispered, "Robert, the rooster, is behind all of this. He's violent, abusive, and darn mean. Stop him if you can!" The two chickens walked closer to the house. Six other chickens joined them, and the group of chickens began to grow outside Mrs. Goose's house. "You'd better leave now, Mr. Majors," she said.

"Well, it is late. I shall head home." He thought, *Robert, my head rooster, is involved with all of this? Just how old is Mrs. Goose?*

Mr. Majors was at dinner when the smell of smoke permeated the air. "Mother, Mother, I smell smoke! Mr. and Mrs. Majors ran outside to see that Mrs. Goose's home was a raging inferno. Mr. Majors ran toward the house and then stopped abruptly. Robert, his rooster, was standing by the charred wreckage of Mrs. Goose's home. Near Robert's feet was a match.

"Robert, is Mrs. Goose dead?"

"I guess so, Mr. Majors. Her house just caught fire. She must be dead." Robert noticed the match at his feet and stepped on it to hide it.

Mr. Majors saw Robert's action but pretended not to notice. "How sad for Mrs. Goose," he said.

"Yes, sir!"

Mr. Majors walked back into the house. Old Blue would guard his wife. He headed into town to buy shotgun shells. As he walked out of the store, he noticed a chicken near his car. He drove home without giving it a second thought. The whole countryside was very quiet. Where were all the animals?

His car traveled around the bend as he approached his farm. He saw smoke coming from the farmhouse. He stepped on the accelerator and sped toward the farm. As he turned in to the farmyard and rounded the corner, two horses kicked the car, sending it into a terrible roll. The loaded shotgun boomed twice.

The shots flew by Mr. Majors' head and went through the windshield. He climbed from the car, only to be confronted by a pack of wild dogs heading straight for him. Without thinking, he reloaded the gun. The gun roared, and the shot hit four of the dogs. Mr. Majors fired again, and the remaining dogs ran away.

Mr. Majors ran toward the farmhouse. Chickens danced in a frenzy around the burning house.

Robert stood there, defiant, as other chickens dragged straw bales toward the house.

Mr. Majors aimed for Robert. The shotgun roared. This shot missed. Robert looked back at Mr. Majors and said, "Don't! We can talk."

Mr. Majors fired again, and Robert fell into the flames.

Mrs. Majors and Old Blue came running from the barn. The house was a blazing inferno. "My dear wife, you are okay! I want you to know that were are going to have the biggest party in town—with all the fried chicken you can eat! I should have listened to the other animals. Robert grew, and my inaction allowed him to grow. First, it was the name-calling, then the bullying and aggression, and finally the violence that led to so many people and animals losing their lives. He had to be stopped." He patted Old Blue and hugged Mrs. Majors.

THE END

8

He's Drinkin' Again

Dude, what's wrong with my parents? They are always at each other! My father comes in from work, and the first thing he wants is his "Chivas on the rocks." When I ask him about drinking a Gatorade, he just slurs, "Son, when a man is in a man's world, he needs manly things."

"But Dad," I say, "why do you have to drink every day? Isn't alcohol a drug? And aren't drugs dangerous?"

"Sure, son, drugs are a scourge of mankind. But this alcohol is sold in stores. Would the government allow something dangerous to your health to be sold in stores?"

"What about cigarettes? *They're* dangerous."

"Peyton, I'm busy. Go see if dinner is ready."

Our conversations end this way all the time. My dad is as thick as a rock! But my mom cries if we fight, so I don't say nothing to the Rock. Sometimes he thinks I am giving him a compliment when I call him "the Rock." Yeah, right. My friends call my dad names—like Boozy, the Vineyard, and some names I just won't repeat.

Dad embarrasses Mom a lot. And you should see him at parties. Wow, he can really dance! But he pinches his dance partners sometimes, and they just slap him. He claims he's drunk, but I'm not sure about that. Still, everyone loves dancing with him.

My grandfather was a musician. He taught my father how to play seven or eight instruments. My grandmother says he learned all those instruments while playing for GIs in the old country during the war.

Being immigrants was hard for my father's family, and I am the only real American of them all. My father and mother are citizens, yeah, but their accents are so thick that they sound weird.

Well, I don't drink, dance, or play any instruments. I don't want to. I will join the army or go to college when I am old enough. This is my family, and I'm stuck with them, but when the time comes, I'm out of here!

THE END

9

Having a Drunk for a Dad Sucks

The teenager sat slumped on a swing, tanned arms wrapped around an orange-wheeled, dirty-brown, scuffed-up skateboard. His hair was a dusty brown, which reminded me of a wig on a white, Styrofoam mannequin's head. He had small, recessed, brown eyes that moved constantly in all directions. He wore small, gold loop earrings in both ears. His shirt was too small, and his blue jeans kept falling down from around his waist. On his stained, olive-green T-shirt were the words, "Make all the dumb people shut up!" Spotted, brown-suede tennis shoes completed the ensemble.

Another young man who looked just like the boy seated on the swing came over and yelled, "Peyton, dude, what's up? Where you been?"

Peyton sat up and mumbled something that was barely audible. It sounded like a cross between a frog and a cow.

"Let's skate!" the other kid shouted. "Come on, Peyton. What's eating you, dude?"

"My dad is drinking again."

"Well, what else is new?"

"Nothin'!" Peyton replied. "Let's go for it." His smile displayed perfect, white teeth and full lips.

He seemed thin and frail as he jumped up, and his pants began to fall again. He grabbed them at the waist, and with amazing agility, he propelled his skateboard forward as he held his pants up.

Peyton passed by me with incredibly fast speed for a skateboard, or so it seemed. His long, brown hair flopped madly in the breeze he left behind.

THE END

10

I Can't Decide

"Peyton!" my mom calls. "Your dinner is ready. I am not going to call you again. What's going to happen when you're in college? The cafeteria won't be open all day!"

"I heard you! I heard you!" I reply. "I'm coming for the dog food."

"Peyton, did you hear your mother?" says my father. "Stop talking stupid, and get down here, now!"

I am seventeen years old. I know a few things! Grown-ups don't know everything. In fact, my dad says some pretty stupid things—things like… oh, I don't know… things like, "Peyton, you should always vote for a Democrat" or "There will never be a woman president."

"Hey, Dad," I say to him, "what about the Queen of England, or what about Margaret Thatcher of Great Britain?"

"That's different!" my dad yells.

My parents are real losers. My mom is an airhead who takes instructions from my dad. She doesn't have any decision-making ability beyond the kitchen. Still, her brain's really valuable. You know why? Because it's never been used.

I know, I know. I'm so cold-blooded. I wish college started tomorrow—or today, actually. Mom and Dad filled out my paperwork for admissions. I can't wait until I'm out of here. My mom and dad went to my same university. Everyone's heard of the University of Texas at Austin. Go, Longhorns! Can you believe those two nerds went to UT?

I can hardly believe I get to go there! It'll be so cool, with Sixth Street and the hike-and-bike trails at Townlake. I have some friends already there, and I can't wait to chill with my boys!

Or maybe not. I have a slight problem. Maybe I shouldn't mention it. Or perhaps I should talk it over with my parents. Yeah, right. Those two couldn't find their way out of a paper bag. My problem is my college roommate.

My best friend, Jamie Steward, is a freshman there. He plays on the football team and is studying engineering. He's not your typical jock. He's smart in school and makes good grades. But here's the problem: Jamie wants me to room with him. I can live in the athletic dorm, because I have an athletic scholarship for track and I made the track team.

Jamie was home the other day, and like old times, he asked me to spend the weekend with his family. I had a nice time… until last night. Last night, Jamie got into my bed, took off his shirt, and tried to give me a back rub. I said no thank you. It irritated me, the whole thing. I don't know what Jamie's up to, but I didn't like it! I didn't feel comfortable. He backed off. Man, I felt like punching his face.

I've decided two things: (1) Jamie's never going to be my college roommate and (2) I'm not speaking to him for a long, long time. Dude! Jamie! What's up? Am I still best friends with him? That's what I can't decide. I've known Jamie forever. We were in pre-K together. I don't know what I'm going to tell the two zookeepers. My parents expect me and Jamie to room together in college. I don't think so! He's my best friend—but he hit on me!

I'd better call him, right now. I've decided that we'll still be friends, and I will definitely go to UT, but as for being roommates—no way!

"Hey, Jamie, man, this is Peyton. No, I ain't mad, but what's up with the shirt off? Oh, I see. You're going through some personal issues—identity issues. Well, I see. That's cool. You have another roommate for the fall semester? Oh. And the two of you are sharing some of the same experiences? No, I'm not hurt at all. But our families were expecting us to keep hanging together. Sure, maybe later. Bye, Jamie."

Well, my problem just settled itself. I'm outta here.

"Peyton, you and Jamie will have fun in college," my dad says.

"I know, Dad." I will have more fun there than here, that's for sure, dude.

"Oh, someone's at the front door," says my mom. "It's probably Margaret. I made a cake for her."

"I'll get it, Mom."

I open the door, and Jamie is standing there. "Jamie, what are you doing here?"

"I don't need an invitation to come over, do I, dude?"

"Peyton, Jamie, get in here!" my dad calls. "Your mom's good cooking is waiting!"

"Peyton, you're my best friend, right, dude?" Jamie says. "I hope I didn't freak you out too much?"

"Jamie, you're still my friend… my best friend. So you want to do something a little different. So what." I am such a liar!

"Well, I'm different now, I think. My interests are kind of new to me. I'm trying to find out who I am. I'm not going to play football next year—not until I figure out some things. I really think I might be gay or something. I'm scared of who I might be! I don't know!"

"Dude, dude, what's new?" I tell him. "College is like that for everyone. It's okay, man. You're still cool with me. Hey, it's life! Me, myself, and I got a lot of doubts and wishes too. But hey, Jamie, I hope you've got my back next year too. Ah… I'm only kidding about getting my back. No, you don't have to laugh! I'm sure that I'll get to know myself a little bit better too."

"Peyton, your dinner's ready!"

"Dude, enough already!" I tell Jamie. "Let's eat! The aliens are calling us earth-dudes for dinner."

THE END

11

Terra and Firma

I was in Miller Park by my house, all by myself. I was sitting there because I had gotten so mad at my baby sister, Lola. She broke the paper spaceship I had worked so hard to put together. It had taken me three whole days to do it. My mom said, "Please remember, Andre, that she is your new baby sister." She said it would be okay if I walked down to the park in our neighborhood just to think for a while and to calm down. So I was sitting there, just thinking how mad I was that Lola, my baby sister, had broken my spaceship.

When I looked up, I couldn't believe my eyes. A tiny spaceship was actually landing on the picnic table. I didn't know if I was seeing things because I was so mad, or if it was real.

The object that was landing was about the size of a basketball. It was steel-colored with a ring of cool, bright, bluish light spinning around it. It had legs like a spider, and it slowly and gently landed right on the picnic table. I reached my hand out to touch it and then screamed. The spaceship thing had shocked me! I was going to knock it over, but then it said, "Sorry! You just touched our force field."

I couldn't believe that the spaceship was talking. It slowed down and eventually stopped glowing. A small door opened on the side nearest me, and two little people about the size of my hand walked out of the spaceship.

They were wearing spacesuits made of a shiny silver material that had the same blue lights circling their waists. That blue light allowed them to fly through the air like hummingbirds. The spacemen flew this way and that way like bumblebees, right in front of my eyes, and I tried to grab one of them. "I wouldn't do that if I were you," said a voice. "You might get the same shock as before." I withdrew my hand quickly, as the painful memory of the first shock surfaced. "My name is Terra," said the voice. "What's yours?"

"I am Andre Swain," I replied. "Are you an alien? What did you say your name was?"

"Ooooahoeraooo," the small man uttered. "Ooooahoeraoo."

The small woman then appeared and repeated a similar sound. "Ooooahoeraoora." A smile appeared on her face.

"I beg your pardon, but I didn't get your names. It sounded like a wolf was howling or a bird was screeching in the night." My face must have seemed like a mask of confusion.

"Well, as I said before, my name is Terra, and this is Firma. We have these nicknames because we visit Earth a lot."

"My name is Andre," I said again. "Welcome to Earth, my home."

"Oh, yes, Andre," said Terra, "Earth is home to lots of humans, and it has been for quite a long time." He looked at a small screen on his wrist. Firma cut in with a sound like a whistle and looked at Terra. He looked back at her and replied with a sound like a ship's foghorn. "I am sorry, Andre," he said, "but it's a long way home, and we will have to leave soon."

"Don't leave now!" I said. "I've never seen an alien before!"

"But I am not an alien, Andre!" Firma shouted. "We have been here a lot! I can't believe this. I just can't believe this. We have been here before, so many times before."

"What she is trying to say," Terra shouted as he walked back and forth on the picnic table, "is that you are not the first person or human we have visited. Firma cannot understand why, in all of our trips here, no one has noticed us or recalled our names. We have spent lots of our resources and energy to come here, and no one ever remembers us. In fact, some humans have been really mean to us upon occasion. We are not going to come back ever again. Do you hear me?" Suddenly both spacemen began to fly back toward the open door of the spaceship.

"Don't go," I pleaded. "Please don't go! Why don't you just make earth your home, and then everyone would know who you are."

The spacemen paused, and Terra said, "Why? We could never leave Erg, our planet. My happiest days are yet to come. I am to become an elder of my people. I could never live here, where there are so many changes and so many different people." He sat down and seemed to be thinking deeply.

"I think that you two would be great here," I said, "but because you are so small, you must be careful that a cat or dog doesn't get you. I promise to tell the whole world that I know you, and then no one will doubt that you exist. No one will doubt you!" I shouted, as I threw my hands up into the air.

Firma had been sitting silently, but she looked up and said, "Andre, we have lived a long time. Terra is older than you think. He is at least two thousand years old. And I—well, I am least one thousand years old. With our recorder on our spaceship, we can easily go back through four or five thousand generations of memory. We have a collective memory that spans time. I suspect that our friends here on earth—and other people we have met—have just passed by us. It's just that we are around forever, but everyone and everything else is changing."

"I won't change," I said. "I will be your unchanging boy."

"Ha! You must change, Andre, and you will," said Firma.

"Please, tell me who are some of the earthmen that you have met?"

"Oh, we have met a lot of different earth men and earth women. Some people have been very nice to us, and some have not. Some years ago, we met a very strange earthman, and he wasn't very nice. He had a weird little mustache and was always sticking his hand into the air. Firma and I thought how strange he was. He seemed to be so controlling and demanding. He insisted that we join his weird parade. When we refused, he threatened to burn our spaceship. We left earth immediately and didn't return for many, many years." Terra shuddered.

"But then we thought we should give earth a second chance," he continued. "We had met so many nice people before that. On our trip back to Earth, we landed smack in the middle of a wrestling mat. You know, Andre, we don't always have perfect control of where we land our spaceship. That's why we named it *Unpredictable*. Anyway, when we landed on the large mat, all we could hear was loud pounding, and we thought, *Uh-oh, trouble*.

"The earthman was very big, but he was so friendly. He told us his name was "The Rock." He said that he might seem mean, but in reality, he was very nice, and the wrestling was all a form of entertainment. He even showed us some moves. Then he winked and said good-bye to us with the lift of an eyebrow. That was just the beginning of all the wonderful people we have encountered on Earth."

"Well, if you can't live on Earth, can you at least come and visit me again sometime?" I asked.

"Andre, we shall come back and see you soon. We promise." Terra and Firma linked hands and walked back into their small spaceship. The band of blue and white light became brighter as the *Unpredictable* moved in a circular motion. The spaceship moved slowly at first, then faster and faster, and in an instant it was gone.

I sat quietly and thought what perhaps a million of earth's people have already thought: *who's gonna believe me anyway?* Oh, well. I had to get back home and face my own little alien, Lola."

THE END

12

Aliens in the Hill Country

I don't think anyone ever thinks about the truth of anything we say. If you say something, I suppose that most people suspect it's just the truth as *you* know it. I am a high school student. I am not a Trekkie or a fan of science fiction literature. I shop at the local grocery store and wait in line like everyone else. I rent my movies from a local video store like all of my friends do. I love pizzas and sodas like everyone else.

But my life is different from my friends' lives. Something happened to me on my grandmother's farm, and I am scared to talk about it with anyone else. I wanted to go to the school counselor, but I'm afraid that my parents will be told or that the rest of the school will find out, and people will think I'm weird. If you find this, and I haven't shared it with you, please don't tell anyone on me.

My grandmother's farm is outside the city where I live. She lives in the Texas hill country near Llano, Texas. Her property is irrigated by a well, and she has a few head of cattle and lots of goats and chickens. We are trying to get her to move to San

Antonio, but she won't come this way. She complains that it's too hot.

Well, anyway, I was sent to Llano to keep her company. I usually hate going, but once you are there, the quiet is pretty calming. I just walk around doing nothing. I feed chickens and sometimes look at my grandmother's herd of three cows. My grandmother is old, and she's retired from working, so three cows are a lot of work. Yesterday, as I was walking outside, it happened.

I was throwing chicken feed to the chickens, when suddenly I had this strange desire to eat roasted chicken. As I was looking at one particular bird, it emitted a laser beam that literally zapped another chicken into a roasted chicken before my eyes. An instant earlier, it had been a chicken with feathers, and suddenly it was a roasted chicken. I just couldn't believe my eyes.

Upon closer inspection, I saw that it wasn't a bird that had zapped the chicken. It was a flying, silver, metallic object about the size of a sixteen-ounce bottle. It seemed that whatever was inside of it was talking to me through my mind, and I knew instantly that this object was going to zap me.

I ran like a rabbit, and a laser bolt almost hit me. I could feel a burning sensation on my arm, something like a sunburn. Immediately a voice in my head said, "Why didn't she die? Get her! Bring that giant down. She knows we are here. Stop her before she alerts others."

I ran into the house as fast as I could and slammed the door. My grandmother was away, thank goodness. I remembered that I had the key to the other car in the garage. Just as I grabbed the key, I saw the metallic object inside the house. This time, it emitted a strange mist that looked like a smoke ring. I had dropped my cell phone, and when the ring encircled it, it shrank!

I ran quickly to the garage, backed the car out, and flew down the highway. I was speeding through the hill country and only slowed down after I hit Highway 281. I drove straight to San Antonio. *Whew*, I thought, *I am watching too much TV.*

When I arrived in my subdivision in San Antonio, I didn't see anything amiss. I went into the house, went straight to the refrigerator, and poured myself a Coke. As I closed the door, a laser flash hit the refrigerator. My reflection in the door had saved me.

I ran around the kitchen island, flung open the microwave door, and immediately hung a right—just escaping another bolt that scorched the kitchen cabinets. I ran around the kitchen island again and stood still in front of the microwave. *Come on, baby*, I thought. *Come after me.*

The object accelerated, and I let it slide past me like a bullet—straight into the microwave. I slammed the door and pushed the maximum power button. The microwave exploded and started a fire. I called 9-1-1, and the firemen came to our house, but I never told anyone what had really happened.

So, if you read this, don't tell anyone, and don't repeat it, or you will have bought a one-way ticket to the crazy house.

My name is Mandy Morrison.

THE END

ABOUT THE AUTHOR

Fryderyk Von Battenburg enjoys writing for children. He loves to write stories which challenge the young reader to ask questions. He hopes that these stories are only the beginning of a lifetime pursuit for knowledge and understanding for the young reader. Fryderyk lives in San Antonio, Texas. Aliens In The Hill Country was written and submitted by India Hays. Thank you India.

ABOUT THE AUTHOR

Fryderyk Von Battenburg enjoys writing for children. He loves to write stories which challenge the young reader to ask questions. He hopes that these stories are only the beginning of a lifetime pursuit for knowledge and understanding for the young reader. Fryderyk lives in San Antonio, Texas. Aliens In The Hill Country was written and submitted by India Hays. Thank you India.

ABOUT THE BOOK

This collection of short stories provides a chance for teenagers to read about current problems or situations that young adults may confront. It's all about having different points of view regarding issues like gender difference and bullying. These stories are great for breaking the ice or for beginning conversations with teenagers that may ease a hurt, comfort someone, or save a life.

www.ingramcontent.com/pod-product-compliance
Lightning Source LLC
LaVergne TN
LVHW041542060526
838200LV00037B/1104